HARRY S. TRUMAN

ENCYCLOPEDIA
of PRESIDENTS

Harry S. Truman

Thirty-Third President of the United States

By Jim Hargrove

Consultant: Charles Abele, Ph.D.
Social Studies Instructor
Chicago Public School System

CHILDRENS PRESS ®

CHICAGO

**Truman shakes hands with newly elected President Eisenhower
on inauguration day, 1953**

Library of Congress Cataloging-in-Publication Data

Hargrove, Jim.
  Harry S. Truman.

  (Encyclopedia of presidents)
  Includes index.
  Summary: Traces the life and political career of the
statesman from Missouri who became president of the
United States following the death of Franklin D.
Roosevelt in 1945.
  1. Truman, Harry S., 1884-1972—Juvenile literature.
2. Presidents—United States—Biography—Juvenile
literature. [1. Truman, Harry S., 1884-1972.
2. Presidents] I. Title. II. Series.
E814.H3   1987   973.918'092'4 [B] [92]   87-11797
ISBN 0-516-01388-2

Picture Acknowledgments

Associated Press/Wide World—14, 17
(2 photos), 20, 21 (2 photos), 29 (bottom), 30,
35, 38, 40, 42, 48, 55, 64, 65, 71, 77, 78, 81, 82,
88

Historical Pictures Service—6, 32, 44, 51
(right), 56, 58

Library of Congress—31

Photri—5

Courtesy Harry S. Truman Library—12, 18, 22,
25, 27, 29 (top), 57

United Press International—4, 8, 10, 16, 39, 43,
45, 46, 51 (left), 60, 61, 62, 63, 68, 70, 72, 73,
75, 79, 84, 85, 86, 87, 89

U.S. Bureau of Printing and Engraving—2

Cover design and illustration by
Steven Gaston Dobson

Truman makes the presidential salute during a flag-raising ceremony in Berlin in 1945. Left to right: General Dwight D. Eisenhower, General George Patton, Truman, Secretary of War Henry Stimson, and General Omar Bradley

Table of Contents

Chapter 1

The Power of the Sun

Late in the afternoon of April 12, 1945, Vice-President Harry Truman stopped by the office of his friend Sam Rayburn, who was the Speaker of the U.S. House of Representatives. As soon as the vice-president arrived, Congressman Rayburn told him that there had been a telephone call from the White House. Steve Early, President Franklin Roosevelt's press secretary, had asked that the vice-president return the call immediately.

When Truman heard Steve Early's strained voice, he suspected that something was wrong. "Please come right over," Early said into his White House telephone, "and come in through the main Pennsylvania Avenue entrance." The vice-president walked quickly out of Sam Rayburn's office, ran through the basement of the Capitol, and on to his car outside. In his haste to get to the White House, the sixty-year-old man lost the Secret Service agents who usually guarded him at all times. He rode in his car the short distance to the White House and walked into the main entrance as requested, rather than the unofficial side entrance he normally used.

Opposite page: The atomic bomb explodes over Japan in 1945

Truman and President Franklin D. Roosevelt having dinner together

As soon as he was inside, he was whisked to the second floor study of Eleanor Roosevelt, the popular and sophisticated wife of the president. Inside the room were the First Lady and her daughter, her daughter's husband, and Steve Early, the man who had first called Truman. Mrs. Roosevelt put her hand on Truman's shoulder and said, "Harry, the president is dead."

After he completed his presidency, Harry Truman wrote about his feelings at this terrible moment, recalling how President Roosevelt's health had been declining during his final months in office. "I was fighting off tears," Truman wrote. "The overwhelming fact that faced me was hard to grasp. I had been afraid for many weeks that something might happen to this great leader, but now the worst had happened and I was unprepared for it."

After a long pause, the new president of the United States asked Mrs. Roosevelt, "Is there anything I can do for you?" The president later wrote that he could never forget the former First Lady's reply.

"Is there anything we can do for you?" she answered, "for you are the one in trouble now." No one could doubt the wisdom of Mrs. Roosevelt's warning.

President Franklin Roosevelt, who had died that very day while trying to rest in Warm Springs, Georgia, had been commanding America's efforts in the final year of World War II. It was the largest war the world had yet seen, and millions of people, from many nations of the world, had already died as a result of it. Although he felt unprepared for the grave responsibilities he now faced, President Truman immediately had to direct American troops against the powerful military forces of Germany and Japan.

For a few minutes, President Truman, Mrs. Roosevelt, and the others stood silently in the White House study. Then there was a knock on the door and the secretary of state entered. Even in such a tragic hour, the work of the government had to continue. It must have surprised many government officials that the new president began to act so quickly.

He ordered an air force plane to take Mrs. Roosevelt to Warm Springs, Georgia. Then he had a car sent for his family — his wife Bess and daughter Margaret — in order to bring them to the White House. Next he telephoned Harlan Stone, the chief justice of the Supreme Court, to come to the White House and give him the oath of office.

Truman takes the oath of office as wife Bess and daughter Margaret look on.

As many government officials rushed to the cabinet room of the White House for their first meeting with the new president, members of the president's staff searched frantically for a Bible needed in the oath-of-office ceremony. Although there were undoubtedly many copies in the White House, it took some time to locate one. Finally, at 7:09 in the evening, Chief Justice Harlan Stone administered the oath to the new president.

For several minutes, official photographs were taken. Then Truman's family and all the government officials left the room, except for the cabinet, the president's closest circle of official advisers. Each cabinet member heads an important department in the executive branch of the government. And the cabinet meets frequently with the president to discuss the problems facing the nation.

President Truman's first cabinet meeting was very brief. But during it, the new president faced his first important decision. Newspaper reporters were asking whether a meeting scheduled for April 25 to establish a new organization called the United Nations would now be canceled. Without hesitating, Truman answered that he would continue the plans Roosevelt had made.

When the brief meeting was over, everyone left the room except for Truman and Secretary of War Henry Stimson. The secretary said that he wanted to speak with the president as soon as possible about a new weapon of "almost unbelievable destructive power." Truman later wrote that "his statement left me puzzled."

April 13, 1945, was Truman's first full day as president of the United States. It didn't take long for many government workers to realize that a remarkably energetic sixty-year-old man had just moved into the White House. Two officials who discovered early what Truman expected of them were Admiral William Leahy and Vice-Admiral Wilson Brown of the U.S. Navy. Both men arrived at the White House at the usual time that day to give reports on the war effort to President Truman, just as they had done for President Roosevelt.

"But on arrival at the White House," Brown wrote later, "I was told by a somewhat flustered assistant that the President had been in his office for well over an hour and was somewhat impatiently waiting for Admiral Leahy and me to make our report. We hastily assembled our papers, hurried over to the Executive Office and were ushered into the President's private office at once."

The attack at Pearl Harbor, December 7, 1941

Both men stood before the new president, ready to give their report standing up, as they had done for President Roosevelt. "For God's sake sit down!" Brown recalled Truman as saying. "You make me nervous! Come around here in the light where I can get a good look at you."

Leahy and Brown made their reports, as did dozens of other military and civilian government officials in the days that followed. The reports indicated that the war in Europe was going well. Within ten days, news arrived that the German Nazi government of Adolph Hitler was prepared to surrender to the Allied forces of America, Russia, Great Britian, and others. But the Japanese government gave no sign of surrendering. On tiny islands in the Pacific Ocean, terrible battles between Allied and Japanese forces were still raging. It was becoming increasingly clear that the Japanese would not surrender until the islands of Japan themselves were invaded.

On April 25, Truman finally found the time to meet with Secretary of War Stimson on the weapon of "almost unbelievable destructive power." Knowing that it would be difficult for Truman to understand what he was about to hear, Stimson prepared a written report that the president could study after the meeting. The report began: "Within four months we shall in all probability have completed the most terrible weapon ever known in human history, one bomb of which could destroy a whole city."

Secretary Stimson was referring to the atomic bomb. In great secrecy, it had been under development in laboratories in Chicago, New York, and Berkeley, California. Huge plants on the West Coast and in Oak Ridge, Tennessee, were preparing critical parts of the bomb, which would be assembled at Los Alamos, New Mexico. The supersecret $2 billion undertaking to develop the atomic bomb was called the "Manhattan Project." The military head of the project, General Leslie Groves, accompanied Secretary Stimson when he met with the president.

During the meeting, Secretary Stimson apparently did most of the talking. He explained the awesome power of the new weapon, and said that, if it worked, it would undoubtedly shorten the war with Japan. Stimson spent much of his time talking about how the bomb could change America's relations with other countries.

In a book about his first year as president, Truman described how this meeting ended: "I thanked him for his enlightening presentation of this awesome subject, and as I saw him to the door I felt how fortunate the country was to have so able and wise a man in its service."

Victims at Hiroshima a few hours after the bomb was dropped

Many historians believe that Truman, like many other people who had heard of the secret project at the time, did not understand the real nature of the atomic bomb. He may well have believed that it was much like the other TNT explosives that had been used throughout the war, only bigger. There is little indication that he understood how fundamentally different it was. The war in Europe was virtually finished. No other nation was close to having a working atomic bomb. Some scientists who understood nuclear energy felt that it should not be necessary to use it in the war. But Truman never seemed to doubt that, if it would shorten the war with Japan and save thousands of American lives, it should indeed be used.

Two months later, Truman left the White House to travel to Potsdam, Germany. There, Allied leaders met to discuss how to govern conquered Germany. The same day that the Potsdam Conference opened, July 16, the United States exploded the world's first atomic bomb in the desert near Alamogordo, New Mexico.

Life in America at the dawn of the Atomic Age was somewhat different than it is now. In 1945, most people learned the news of the day by reading newspapers or listening to newscasts on the radio. In a few cities — such as New York, Philadelphia, Chicago, and San Francisco — a few thousand people watched flickering black-and-white programs on a new system called television. But it was years before most U.S. households had television sets.

Although commercial airline travel was not uncommon, the vast majority of people still traveled, even long distances, in cars, buses, trains, and ships. Airline travel was still considered somewhat hazardous. Many people, both women and men, wore hats, even in warm weather. Also in 1945, the world's first electronic digital computer, ENIAC, was being built at the University of Pennsylvania. Although it weighed twenty-seven tons and filled an entire room, ENIAC was less powerful than one of today's $200 microcomputers.

This was America when, on August 6, 1945, the American B-29 bomber *Enola Gay* dropped an atomic bomb over the Japanese city of Hiroshima. Truman, aboard the American ship *Augusta* on his way home from the Potsdam Conference, was given the news of the awesome attack. He issued a statement declaring: "The force from which the sun draws its power has been loosed against those who brought war to the Far East."

Rescue workers in Nagasaki carry a body through the ruins.

Three days later, the power of the sun once again visited Japan. The American Superfortress airplane "No. 77" dropped a different kind of atomic bomb, with the same devastating effect, over the Japanese city of Nagasaki. The next day the Japanese government, whose flag pictured a rising sun, surrendered. World War II was over. A wondrous and frightening new age had begun.

Harry Truman lived for twenty years after he left the presidency. When he died at the age of eighty-eight in 1972, American astronauts had already walked on the moon. But when he was born in 1884, he entered a world of mules and horse-drawn carriages.

Above: The Japanese surrender delegation stands before General Douglas MacArthur.
Below: MacArthur hands the pen to General Jonathan Wainright after signing.

Chapter 2

Little Four-Eyes

In 1887, John Anderson Truman and Martha Young Truman moved with their infant son Harry to a six-hundred-acre farm owned by Martha's family. The farm was in the state Missouri, about seventeen miles south of Kansas City. In dry weather, the dirt road that passed through the Young farm, as it was known, gave a solid enough surface for the horses, mules, and wagons that traveled it. In wet weather, mud made the going worse.

Some years later, a railroad builder constructed a line between Kansas City and Springfield, Missouri. A station was built along the tracks about a mile south of the Young farm. Because the station was on a high point of land with a splendid view for miles in all directions, it was called Grandview. Soon people began calling the large farm near the station the Grandview farm.

Harry S. Truman was born in the Missouri town of Lamar on the afternoon of May 8, 1884. (Harry had no middle name. His parents gave him the initial "S" so that both grandfathers could claim him as their namesake.) He often recalled how his grandfather drove him to a fair near Grandview in a horse-drawn cart with two big wheels.

Opposite page: Harry at around the age of eight   19

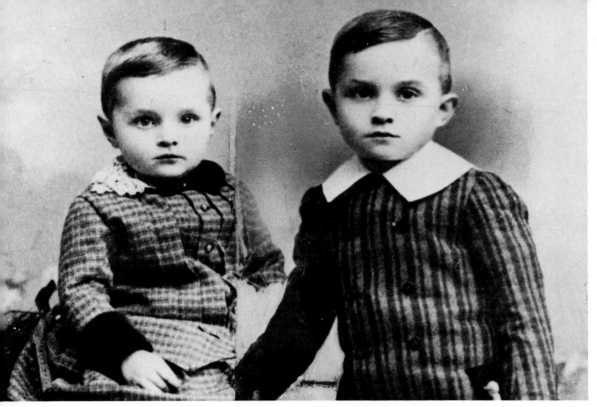

Harry at four (right), with his brother Vivian, age two

Other fond memories included rides around the Grandview farm on a Shetland pony with a beautiful saddle and hours spent playing in the cornfields and mud holes. Of course, there were chores to do on the farm as well, and even young children were expected to help out with the work. One chore that Harry faced at an unusually young age was learning how to read. By the time he was five years old, his mother had taught him how to read simple sentences in the newspaper and the family Bible.

Harry had a brother named Vivian who was two years younger. In 1890, shortly after Harry's sister Mary Jane was born, the Truman family moved to the little town of Independence, Missouri, just east of Kansas City. Although in later years Harry worked on the Grandview farm for an extended time, he always saw Independence as his home.

Above: Truman's birthplace in Lamar, Missouri
Below: The Truman home in Independence, Missouri

Elizabeth (Bess) Wallace at the age of four

Harry later wrote: "With our barns, chicken house, and a grand yard in which to play, all the boys and girls in the neighborhood for blocks around congregated at our house. We always had ponies and horses to ride, goats to hitch to our little wagon. . . . We would harness two red goats to the little wagon and drive it everywhere around the place."

One of the neighborhood farm children who became friends with Harry was a pretty young girl with curly golden hair and bright blue eyes. Her name was Elizabeth Wallace, but everyone called her Bess. Harry and Bess eventually got married, but they hardly rushed into it. He was thirty-five and she was thirty-four.

Harry began attending public school in 1892, somewhat late considering that he was already eight years old. Nevertheless, the head start his mother had given him at home helped to make school an easy experience for him.

Although Harry already knew how to read when he began his schooling, he found it difficult to read the small print in newspapers and books. A visit to an eye doctor resulted in a pair of thick new glasses and a stern warning about the dangers to the eye of broken glass. "I was so carefully cautioned by the eye doctor about breaking my glasses and injuring my eyes," Harry wrote years later, "that I was afraid to join in the rough-and-tumble games in the schoolyard and back lot."

Glasses, especially those worn by a youngster, were an unusual sight in Independence during the 1890s. Some of the kids in the area made fun of them, referring to Harry, who was never very big, as "little four-eyes." Instead of joining their games, Harry spent his free time reading. "By the time I was thirteen or fourteen years old," he wrote, "I had read all the books in the Independence Public Library and our big old Bible three times through." He particularly enjoyed reading books about history. "The only thing new in the world," he once said, "is the history you don't know."

Despite a severe case of diphtheria during his second year at school—which left his legs, arms, and throat paralyzed for months—Harry was an excellent student. He skipped the third grade entirely. Good grades also marked his career in high school, where he continued to be most interested in history, especially the lives of famous people.

While still in high school, he began to work at his first paying job. At a salary of $3 a week, he had to open up Jim Clinton's drugstore at 6:30 each morning.

Mr. Clinton kept whiskey bottles in a little cabinet under the prescription case. Early each morning, a group of men arrived at the drugstore to buy little glasses of the alcohol for ten cents each. They hid behind the prescription case to drink, so that passersby on the sidewalk could not see them. There were a number of saloons in the center of town where some of the leading citizens of Independence stopped for a morning drink. But the men who drank whiskey as they hid in Clinton's Drug Store were afraid for people to see them. All his life, Harry tried to avoid such phoniness—in himself as well as in others.

Harry Truman graduated from high school in 1901, shortly after his seventeenth birthday. He hoped to continue his education at the U.S. Naval Academy in Annapolis, Maryland, or the U.S. Military Academy in West Point, New York. Unfortunately, army officers in Kansas City told him that his poor eyesight would keep these dreams from coming true. To make matters worse, his father lost most of his savings trading in grains, so now even an education at a regular college was an impossibility.

Instead, Harry got a job working as an accountant for crews building the Santa Fe railroad. A year later, he and his brother Vivian began working as clerks in a Kansas City bank. Both men lived in a Kansas City boarding house, where another boarder named Arthur Eisenhower lived. Arthur's brother Dwight later became president right after Harry's term.

Harry in his National Guard uniform

Harry Truman was an excellent bank clerk and was popular with his fellow employees. When he began working at the bank in 1902, his salary was $35 a month. By 1904, he was earning $125 each month, an excellent income for the time. The following year, 1905, he joined the National Guard of Missouri, becoming an original member of the newly formed Battery B. He worked with the National Guard only once in a while, but had to pay twenty-five cents each week for the privilege.

Despite his great success in the banking field, Harry left Kansas City to return to the Grandview farm the very next year, in 1906. His father was helping his mother's family run the large farm. When several older members of the Young family died, John Truman asked his son for help. Harry quickly agreed, moving back to the farm where he had spent a few happy years as a child. He remained on the farm for more than a decade, proving that he was as good a farmer as he had been a bank clerk. When his father died a few years later, Harry became the chief manager of the farm. Soon, income from the Grandview farm was around $15,000 a year, extremely high for those days.

By 1915, virtually all of America was being transformed by a relatively new device—the automobile. Across the country, mules and horse-drawn carriages were being replaced by the noisy new machines. And just as suddenly, there was a huge demand for petroleum to make the gasoline that the clanking machines devoured. In Oklahoma, Kansas, and Missouri, oil men were drilling thousands of deep wells into the prairie, sometimes finding rich deposits of oil for the fabulous new market.

Harry Truman was now the manager and part owner of a highly successful farm. With money to spare, he looked for places to invest it. In 1916, he invested $5,000 in an Oklahoma oil partnership. The company was preparing to drill some test wells in Oklahoma, but there was a sudden shortage of workers, and it was unable to do so. When others drilled the same land some years later, they discovered the Teter Oil Pool, one of the richest oil deposits in the central United States.

Truman right before his induction into the army

The reason for the manpower shortage in 1916 was as simple as it was serious. World War I was already raging in Europe. By the following year, the United States declared war — first on Germany, and then on Austria-Hungary. All across the nation, American men were joining the military to fight in the huge, bloody war.

Because of his experience in the National Guard, Harry Truman became a first lieutenant in the 35th Infantry Division of the U.S. Army. Before leaving for France on the S.S. *George Washington*, Lieutenant Truman bought three spare pairs of glasses from a patriotic eyeglass maker who refused payment. But when he arrived in France, he found that the soldiers under his command were hardly so friendly. Some weren't ready to take orders from him.

"I didn't come here to get along with you," he bluntly told the men. "You've got to get along with me. If there are any of you who can't, speak up right now and I'll bust your back right now." After that, the soldiers found that they could indeed take orders from their new commander.

Before long, Truman was promoted to captain. He and his men were soon involved in some huge, bloody battles in the final year of the war. Captain Truman, or "Captain Harry" as he was known to his men, proved himself an excellent military commander. But in the heat of battle, he tended to swear a lot. "I never heard a man cuss so well or intelligently," a soldier who watched him in action recalled, "and I'd shooed a million mules."

World War I was over when, on May 6, 1919, Major Harry Truman was discharged from the army. At the age of thirty-five, he wasted little time getting on with his private life. On June 28, he married his childhood sweetheart, Bess, at a ceremony in Independence.

Instead of going back to farming, Harry decided to open up a store in downtown Kansas City. With a friend named Eddie Jacobson, he sold men's hats and ties and other small items. This type of store, which used to be called a haberdashery, isn't seen much any more. The Truman & Jacobson Haberdashery was seen for only two years in Kansas City. In 1922, after a recession hit the country, the store failed, leaving Truman and Jacobson deeply in debt.

Jacobson declared bankruptcy so that he wouldn't have to repay the money he owed. But Harry Truman refused to walk away from his debts; he took fifteen years to repay them. In the meantime, he entered the world of politics.

Above: Harry and Bess on their wedding day
Below: Harry (left) in his Kansas City haberdashery

Above: Truman's parents, John Anderson Truman and Martha Young Truman, on their wedding day in 1882. Opposite page: Harry Truman with wife Bess and daughter Margaret

Chapter 3

The Senator from Pendergast

In 1922, when Harry Truman began his political career, there were only two serious political parties in Kansas City. One was the Democratic party. The other was . . . *another* Democratic party. At the time, the only thing expected of Republican politicians was for them to be defeated by Democrats. It was difficult to find a single Republican who failed to live up to that expectation.

With so many Democrats at hand, the party naturally split into two (and later even more) different groups. One group was nicknamed the Rabbits, the other, the Goats. The Goats were led by a boss named Tom Pendergast, a heavy-set politician who enjoyed betting on horse races. Tom Pendergast's most important assistant was his brother Mike. Mike had a son named Jim, who had served in the same infantry group as Harry during World War I.

When Jim Pendergast learned that his father and his uncle were searching for a candidate for county judge, he suggested Harry Truman. In Missouri, a county judge was a real politician. In Kansas City's Jackson County, for instance, the three county judges set taxes, established budgets for road construction, and oversaw a number of county institutions.

At a meeting of Jackson County Democratic township leaders in 1922, Mike Pendergast followed his son's advice and recommended Harry for the office of county judge. Pendergast said that Truman was a returned soldier, a captain "whose men didn't want to shoot him."

In order to win in Jackson County, all Harry had to do was to win the Democratic nomination. Victory against the Republican candidate in the election was practically certain. Truman, one of the Goats, managed to defeat the Rabbit candidate, a wealthy banker, by about three hundred votes. The angry Rabbit leader remarked that the people "preferred a busted merchant to a prosperous banker." But Harry turned the issue around. "Most people were broke," he wrote, "and they sympathized with a man in politics who admitted his position."

Democrats, including Harry Truman, won every election in Jackson County in 1922. During the two years he served as a county judge, he claimed that he became "completely familiar with every road and bridge in the county." But despite his hard work, he lost his bid for reelection in 1924. Members of the Ku Klux Klan helped to defeat him. It was the only election he lost until the end of his presidency. Better news came the same year with the birth of a daughter, Margaret, the Trumans' only child.

Because he now had a family to support, Truman had to work at a number of different jobs to make ends meet. But, having served a single term in a political office, he was already fascinated by politics. While considering candidates to run in the 1926 elections, Tom Pendergast gave Harry the nod to run for chief judge of Jackson County.

Truman (right) in Kansas City in 1924 with Robert L. Hood

Candidate Truman campaigned by promising to improve the poorly paved roads that slowed down automobile traffic throughout much of the county. Voters in Jackson County must have felt that this was an important issue. Truman easily won the nomination and, of course, the election, keeping the position for the next eight years.

Judge Truman was true to his campaign words. He worked tirelessly to raise the millions of dollars needed to resurface the roads, and then made sure that the money was spent wisely. As the nation prospered during the 1920s, the roads in Jackson County were vastly improved. The judge also saw to it that money was spent wisely to build two new courthouses and a hospital. Although he had a job that involved passing out millions of dollars, Truman was always completely honest in the way he did business. The same could not be said of the Pendergasts.

Tom and Mike Pendergast ran their Democratic machine by helping people get offices and then expecting political "favors" from them in return. At least once while he was chief judge of Jackson County, Truman discovered what a favor for the Pendergasts meant. Tom Pendergast called him and asked him to come to a meeting. At the meeting were a number of construction bosses who didn't like the way Judge Truman awarded construction contracts. They felt that they should be given the money to do the work, especially since they were such good friends of Boss Tom Pendergast.

Judge Truman disappointed everyone at the meeting. He told Pendergast's buddies that they might indeed be able to get work on county jobs. But they would have to submit bids just like everyone else. Then, their bids would have to be the lowest, so that the county could save as much money as possible. Finally, in order to be paid, they would have to complete the job exactly as it had been planned. Apparently, this was not what the gathering wanted to hear. According to Truman, Pendergast said at the end of the meeting, "I told you he's the contrariest cuss in the state of Missouri." Surprisingly, Truman once stated that Pendergast never interfered with his work as an honest county judge.

In 1930, shortly after America fell into the Great Depression, Judge Truman was reelected by a huge majority. Now, as he traveled over Jackson County's fine road system, he saw a disturbing sight at almost every town he visited. Large groups of unemployed men were standing in long lines waiting for welfare checks.

As the early years of the Great Depression went by, the Pendergast machine in Kansas City became even more corrupt. Boss Tom began working with a hoodlum named Johnny Lazia. Before long, Pendergast's organization had a hand in a variety of illegal operations, including prostitution and gambling. When a more honest Democratic organization challenged the Pendergasts, four of the challengers were killed and many others were beaten brutally by Lazia's thugs.

Boss Tom had crushed his opposition. But now many people realized that he was little more than a common criminal. When it was time for him to choose his candidate for the U.S. Senate, many people refused the offer, not wanting to be associated with the Pendergasts.

On May 15, 1934, one week after his fiftieth birthday, Judge Truman received word that one of the Pendergasts, Jim, wanted to meet with him. At the meeting, Harry learned that he was being offered the chance to run for the U.S. Senate with the backing of the Pendergast machine, a mixed blessing at best.

Since he was completely unknown outside of Jackson County, Truman understood instantly that the Pendergasts were using his good reputation to meet their own needs. On the other hand, he thought, this was an opportunity that might never come again. Without giving an answer, Harry went home and discussed the opportunity with Bess, who, he always said, was the real boss in his life. Although Bess wanted to stay in Independence, she encouraged her husband to try for the Senate if that was what he really wanted. The next day, he accepted.

Truman holds a Canadian goose bagged during a Missouri River hunting trip the first autumn after his 1935 election to the Senate.

The greatest challenge, again, was to win the Democratic nomination. Other Democrats, ashamed of the Pendergasts' disgraceful reputation, put up their own candidates. Many people thought that Truman had little chance to win. Realizing that he faced an uphill battle, he campaigned tirelessly, making a dozen or more speeches in a single day. Although many people were suspicious of the Pendergasts' backing, none could find even a hint of dishonesty in his work as a county judge. He eventually won the nomination and, as did many Democrats throughout the country, easily defeated his Republican opponent.

On January 3, 1935, with Bess and ten-year-old Margaret sitting in the visitors' gallery, Harry Truman was sworn in to the U.S. Senate. But many people distrusted the freshman senator because of his association with the Pendergasts. Instead of calling him the senator

Senator Truman in the kitchen with his wife, Bess, whom he called "The Boss." She liked her toast dark.

from Missouri, some of his critics referred to him as the senator from Pendergast. "When you're in politics, you've got to be elected," Truman once said in his own defense. "You can't be unless the people who control the votes are for you. But when you have a good reputation and are a good vote getter, the people who control the votes are more likely to be for you."

After his haberdashery failed, Harry Truman was never a particularly wealthy man. Although some politicians found ways to become rich while they were in office, Truman did not. While other senators and congressmen lived in large homes and had servants, the Trumans lived in a small apartment just off Connecticut Avenue in Washington. Bess did all the cooking and even typed her husband's letters to save the expense of hiring a secretary.

Tom Pendergast (right) receives a medal from an Italian organization.

Despite his sincere honesty, it took many of the other senators years to accept Harry as one of their own. Only a few were kind to their shy new colleague from the beginning. One was Ham Lewis of Illinois, who told him, "For the first six months you'll wonder how you got here, and after that you'll wonder how the rest of us got here." Such words must have been a comfort as Truman's hard work and support for Roosevelt's New Deal only gradually won him more trust and support. Just a few senators were still suspicious of the senator from Pendergast when, in 1939, the Pendergasts nearly ended his political career.

That year, Tom Pendergast's fondness for horse racing and corruption finally got him in trouble with the law. He was accused of accepting three-quarters of a million dollars in bribes from insurance companies and of gambling away more than half of it. With little defense, he pleaded guilty and was sentenced to a year in jail.

With its leader facing a jail term, the Pendergast machine was finally smashed beyond repair. By 1940, many people were interested in running for Truman's Senate seat. To make matters worse, Senator Truman refused to support the reelection of the man who was prosecuting Pendergast. He did so because he was angered about not being asked his opinion about the election. But to many people, it appeared as if he were trying to protect a corrupt old politician who had helped him.

Harry Truman began his uphill battle to retain his Senate seat by making two campaign pledges: to support the New Deal policies of President Roosevelt and to help to build up America's defenses. He thought this was necessary because World War II had already begun in Europe.

Through hard work and a number of tricky but honest political deals, Truman managed to win the Democratic nomination in a very close primary vote. He also won the election to keep his Senate seat, but this time by only 44,000 votes, down from a quarter of a million six years earlier. It was a close election, but Harry Truman had finally proved that he was capable of winning without the help of the Pendergast machine. When he returned to the Senate after his reelection, many of the other senators applauded him warmly.

In his second term in the U.S. Senate, Truman finally managed to establish a national reputation as an honest and worthy politician. During this time, he served his country as well as any other senator ever had. He also proved, as he had before, that he could be counted upon to keep his campaign promises.

Senator Truman inspects a Baltimore bomber plant.

When Congress convened in January of 1941, much of Europe had already been conquered by the German armies of Adolph Hitler. Many politicians felt that it was only a matter of time before America would be drawn into the Second World War. Throughout 1941, both houses of Congress passed many bills calling for huge amounts of money to be spent to build up America's military defenses.

Few politicians understood better than Harry Truman how huge amounts of money could be wasted by people working on government contracts. Since his days as a Missouri county judge, he had devised ways of seeing to it that tax dollars were spent wisely. It was only natural,

Truman with Thomas G. Corcoran, who testified before Truman's committee

then, that in February of 1941 he formally suggested that the Senate establish a special committee to investigate defense spending.

When the committee was approved, and given a tiny budget of $15,000, Truman became its chairman. The official name of the new group was the Senate Defense Investigating Committee. But in just a few weeks, people all over America were calling it the Truman Committee. Almost immediately, members of the Truman Committee found ways for the government to get more and better equipment for its money. It even found ways to speed up the defense buildup.

John L. Lewis,
president of the
United Mine Workers,
demands that
Congress enforce
safety measures for
miners.

In the spring of 1941, members of the United Mine Workers went out on strike because they felt their wages weren't high enough. The coal that these workers mined was vital to America's national defense. During a meeting with United Mine Workers' leader John L. Lewis and several management groups, Truman discovered that only the mine operators in some southern states refused to come to an agreement with the workers. In an angry message to the southerners, Truman threatened that unless coal was being mined within twenty-four hours, he would bring them all before his committee "to show why their wage dispute should come ahead of the national safety." The strike ended that very night.

Truman presiding over a defense committee investigation

Quickly, the budget of the Truman Committee was increased so that more investigators could be hired. Before long, Truman and his staff were investigating factories and businesses all over the country. Huge defense contracts were rewritten as a result of Truman Committee recommendations. When the group found that the defense buildup would cause an aluminum shortage, a massive new aluminum production program was begun.

The committee even showed that a major overhaul of an executive agency, the Office of Production Management, was badly needed. It was replaced by the War Production Board, which operated much more efficiently along the lines suggested by the Truman Committee.

Allied troops coming ashore on the North African coast

"I'm tired as a dog and having the time of my life," Harry wrote home to Bess. He was also providing a wonderful service to his country. By the time the Japanese air force attacked Pearl Harbor on December 7, 1941, the U.S. Congress had already approved spending more than $16 billion to make America ready for war. Much of that incredible sum might have been wasted, leaving America not as well prepared for the struggle ahead, had it not been for the work of the Truman Committee.

After the U.S. entered the fighting, Truman had to work even harder. His committee discovered that much needed steel and metals were being turned into children's toys instead of weapons for the national defense. It pointed out other facts that made Americans think seriously about the war in which their country was involved. Even though the navy wanted to keep the fact secret, the Truman Committee explained to the public that a higher tonnage of American ships were sunk by German U-boats in 1942 than were produced throughout the nation.

Part of the reason for the committee's success was the fact that its chairman was not afraid to step on anyone's toes. There was only one time that Truman called off an investigation as a result of a request by a politician. In 1943, Truman Committee investigators drove up to the gate of a huge new plant being built near Oak Ridge, Tennessee. The investigators demanded to know what the plant was making. When they were not given an answer, Truman began demanding answers in Washington.

Finally, Secretary of War Henry Stimson explained that the Oak Ridge plant was part of a top secret project, "the greatest project in the history of the world." The secretary pleaded with Senator Truman to call off his investigation. Truman, this one time, agreed. Although he knew little about it, it was his first inkling of the Manhattan Project and the atomic bomb.

By 1944, the tide of war was shifting to the side of the United States and its allies. But 1944 was also an election year, and toward the end of it there was a terrific surprise in store for Senator Truman.

Harry Truman waving to Democratic convention delegates in Chicago
after his nomination as vice-president on July 21, 1944

Chapter 4

The Fast Road
to the White House

In the presidential election year of 1944, there was little doubt that Franklin Roosevelt was the choice of a majority of Americans. His famous "New Deal" had led the country out of the worst depression in its history. As commander-in-chief of the armed forces, he had helped American armies make gains against the enemy.

Vice-President Henry Wallace, however, was a more controversial figure. There were rumors that President Roosevelt might prefer someone else as his vice-presidential running mate in the upcoming elections.

Among the names mentioned was that of Harry S. Truman, although he later wrote that he had little interest in the vice-presidency: "I was doing the job I wanted to do; it was the one I liked, and I had no desire to interrupt my career in the Senate. As the time for the Democratic Convention drew closer, however, my name was mentioned frequently as a possible candidate for the nomination. This disturbed me, for I had repeatedly given notice that I did not want to be a candidate."

Political conventions are an important part of the lengthy process to elect both presidents and vice-presidents. Each summer during a presidential election year, representatives, called delegates, from various political parties in every state meet to select a presidential and vice-presidential candidate for their party. The Republican and Democratic conventions attract the most interest, since these two parties, at least in recent times, have been the most powerful. Harry Truman was one of the men selected to represent the Democratic party of Missouri at the 1944 Democratic National Convention.

Shortly before he left for the convention, Senator Truman received a phone call from a man named James Byrnes. Byrnes was a skillful public servant who had given up his lifetime position as a justice of the Supreme Court in order to become an aide for President Roosevelt during the war. Now, Byrnes said over the phone, the president wanted him as his vice-presidential running mate. He asked Truman to nominate him at the convention. "I told him that I would be glad to do it if the President wanted him as a running mate," Truman later wrote.

Many Democrats were interested in becoming candidates for vice-president that summer. Soon after the call from Byrnes, an important Democratic senator telephoned Truman asking if he would be willing to nominate him at the convention. Harry explained that he had already agreed to nominate James Byrnes.

Truman traveled to Chicago, where the Democratic National Convention was scheduled to open July 19. In Chicago, he met with at least three labor leaders who had

Left: Vice-President Henry Wallace. Right: James Byrnes

important voices in the Democratic party at the time. All three men said that they were opposed to the nomination of incumbent Vice-President Henry Wallace, as well as James Byrnes. Instead, they preferred Supreme Court Justice William O. Douglas or Truman himself.

Before long, Maryland's two senators said that their state's delegation was solidly behind Truman for the nomination. Senator Truman explained the new developments to Byrnes, who told him just to wait, and that "the President would straighten everything out in plenty of time." But on Tuesday, July 18, the evening before the convention began, Democratic National Chairman Bob Hannegan had a brief meeting with Truman. Harry Truman, according to Hannegan, was President Roosevelt's choice to be vice-president. Harry could hardly believe his ears. Unaware that Hannegan had personally met with Roosevelt, Truman thought he must have been mistaken.

51

"Bob, look here," Truman told Hannegan. "I don't want to be Vice-President. I bet I can go down the street and stop the first ten men I see and that they can't tell me the names of two of the last ten Vice-Presidents of the United States."

The pressure to accept the nomination increased when the Missouri delegates first met in Chicago. Truman was immediately elected chairman of the delegation. When the other delegates suggested that his own name be placed in nomination for vice-president, Harry explained that it could not be, because he was not a candidate.

The other Missouri delegates, however, refused to take no for an answer. Someone at the meeting tricked Harry into going to the door of the meeting room, supposedly to check on a visitor who wanted to enter. Quickly, the delegates voted to name Harry Truman as their candidate for the vice-presidential nomination.

Senator Truman now knew that delegates from at least two states planned to nominate him. But he still did not believe that the president really wanted him.

More than a thousand Democratic delegates from every state in the country crowded into Chicago Stadium when the Democratic National Convention opened on Wednesday, July 19. The popular support to renominate President Roosevelt was overwhelming. The real question concerned who would become his running mate. When the time came to vote for president, Roosevelt won easily in the first round. Out of a total of 1,176 votes, he gathered 1,086. The questions now turned to the vice-presidential nomination, which would be decided on Friday.

On Thursday afternoon, Democratic Chairman Bob Hannegan called Senator Truman to a meeting at the Blackstone Hotel in downtown Chicago. When he arrived, a number of Democratic leaders began to put pressure on him to accept a vice-presidential nomination. But surprising as it may seem, Truman still did not want to become vice-president. He simply enjoyed his work in the Senate too much. But once again, the Democrats around him would not take no for an answer.

While the meeting was in progress, Hannegan placed a long-distance phone call to President Roosevelt, who at the time was in San Diego, California. The president always spoke loudly into the phone, usually making it possible for a number of people at the other end of the line to hear him clearly. When Hannegan and President Roosevelt began talking, Harry easily could hear both sides of the conversation.

"Bob," the president said to Hannegan, "have you got that fellow lined up yet?"

"No," Hannegan answered. "He is the contrariest Missouri mule I've ever dealt with."

"Well you tell him," the president shouted, "if he wants to break up the Democratic party in the middle of a war, that's his responsibility." The president slammed down his telephone, ending the conversation abruptly.

Truman later wrote about his feelings during the incident. "I was completely stunned," he wrote. "I sat for a minute or two and then got up and began walking around the room. All the others were watching me and not saying a word.

" 'Well,' I said finally, 'if that is the situation, I'll have to say yes, but why the hell didn't he say so in the first place.' "

With the popular president solidly behind him, Senator Truman easily won the vice-presidential nomination on the second ballot that Friday. Huge, happy demonstrations followed his nomination and his short acceptance speech. After the speech, which he made with Bess and daughter Margaret at his side, police had to form a human wall to protect the Truman family from the surging, cheering crowd. Yelling to be heard above the din, Bess asked her husband, "Are we going to have to go through this all the rest of our lives?"

Because he was saving his strength to oversee America's war effort, the president asked his running mate to do all the campaigning. Harry Truman traveled all over the country making campaign speeches, but it was never much of a fight. When election day came in November of 1944 the Roosevelt-Truman team won by more than three-and-a-half million votes.

It snowed on January 20, 1945, when Vice-President Truman stood next to President Roosevelt at the White House to be sworn into office. For only the third time in American history, a president and vice-president were inaugurated while the nation was at war. During a luncheon following the ceremony, Truman slipped away and "hitchhiked" a ride to the Capitol. There, he telephoned his old mother at Grandview. "Now you behave yourself," she told the new vice-president of the United States.

President Roosevelt and Vice-President-Elect Truman after the 1944 election

For a few months, Truman performed the limited duties of the vice-president. He served as president of the Senate, although even those responsibilities are limited. At the president's request, he attended the few cabinet meetings that were held in the early months of 1945. But Vice-President Truman held his office for less than three months. On April 12, his friend Sam Rayburn told him of that urgent call from the White House. The man who didn't want to become vice-president now was forced to be president.

Above: Photographers snap away on Truman's first day as president.
Opposite page: The picture of Bess that Truman kept in the Oval Office

President Harry Truman giving a radio address from his office

Chapter 5

Thirty-Third President
of the United States

"Boys, if you ever pray, pray for me now," the new president told White House reporters during his first full day in office.

"Good luck, Mr. President," one of the them shouted.

"I wish you hadn't called me that," the president answered sadly. He knew, and everyone else feared, that taking over Franklin Roosevelt's job would be a very difficult task. No president in American history had served as long as Roosevelt had. Few had enjoyed such lasting popularity. In the midst of the largest war in the history of the world, Harry Truman had to take over the responsibilities of the mighty Franklin D. Roosevelt—with no warning at all.

During the early weeks of his presidency, many people found it almost impossible to believe that Roosevelt was gone. But from the beginning, Truman let it be known that he was the new man in charge of the White House. Once he called a friend, a former member of Roosevelt's cabinet, to tell him that "the president" had appointed a man to an important position in the government.

Truman kept this sign,
"The Buck Stops Here,"
on his desk in
the Oval Office
while he was president.

"Did the president make that appointment before he died?" the friend asked Truman.

"No," Truman replied, "he made it just now."

The people who worked with President Harry Truman quickly realized that America had found a surprisingly strong and intelligent new leader. But millions of American citizens took much longer to reach the same conclusion. President Truman was hardly surprised by his slow acceptance, and he seldom backed away from a struggle. "If you can't stand the heat," he once said, "stay out of the kitchen."

On his large desk, he kept two sayings printed on small plaques. One said: "The buck stops here." The other had a saying by Mark Twain: "Always do right. This will gratify some people and astonish the rest."

Truman watches U.S. delegates sign the United Nations charter in San Francisco.

One of the first things Harry Truman did when he became president was to help establish the United Nations. As Russian troops were advancing westward toward Germany in the final months of the war, they set up governments in the conquered countries that would be sure to follow instructions from Moscow. At a San Francisco conference to establish the United Nations organization, many Allied governments refused to allow membership to Poland because Russia had not allowed free elections to take place there. Russia insisted that Poland should be given membership in the UN, and threatened to abandon the organization if it were refused. Without Russia, the world's largest country, the UN would certainly fail.

Andrei Gromyko, Russian ambassador to the U.S., signs the UN charter.

President Truman was angered by the government the Russians had set up in Poland. In agreements with other Allied nations, Russia had agreed to allow democratic elections in nations it captured from the Nazi government of Adolf Hitler. Now, the Russians were failing to live up to their promises. And their broken promises were threatening the existence of the United Nations.

At a White House meeting with Russia's foreign minister, Vyacheslav Molotov, and its ambassador to America, Andrei Gromyko, Truman hotly criticized Russian foreign policy in Eastern Europe. "I have never been talked to in my life like this," Molotov complained.

"Carry out your agreements," the president replied hotly, "and you won't get talked to like this." The Russians never did carry out their agreements exactly, but a

Truman at the Potsdam Conference with Winston Churchill and Joseph Stalin

compromise was made allowing Poland to enter the United Nations. But the Russians' policy of establishing governments friendly to them in Eastern Europe, regardless of the true feelings of the people in those countries, was the beginning of what would later be called the "Cold War."

In July 1945, in Potsdam, Germany, a meeting was held to determine the political structure of Europe after the defeat of Nazi Germany. There Truman met with the other two leaders of the "Big Three" Allied nations, Winston Churchill of Great Britain and Joseph Stalin of the Soviet Union. President Truman, who stood five feet, nine inches tall, was greatly amused by the fact that he was the tallest of the "Big Three" leaders.

Representatives of
German and Allied
nations meet in
Reims, France. The
three German
representatives are
seated at left with
their backs to the
camera.

General Gustaf Jodl, German chief of staff (center) signs the terms of Germany's unconditional surrender in Reims, France, on May 7, 1945. With him are his personal aide, Major General Wilhelm Oxenius (left), and General Admiral Hans von Friedburg (right), commander in chief of the German navy.

When Japanese leaders ignored warnings of the devastating new weapon, the two atomic bombs were dropped and World War II was over. Americans and many other people were jubilant, but for President Harry Truman, a new battle was about to begin.

Throughout his life, Truman was fascinated by history. History clearly showed him that, following a war, the American economy was quite predictable. First, there was a business boom as people bought all kinds of goods they had gone without during wartime. But since factories had been busy building guns and other equipment of war, there was always a shortage of the very items wanted most by consumers.

With quantities scarce, prices would rise. Faced with higher prices, people would be able to buy less. With less demand from consumers, American factories would have to produce fewer products and lay off workers. As surely as night followed day, Truman knew, a business boom led to a bust soon after a war was over.

In order to avoid the economic mistakes of the past, President Truman proposed a series of new laws. He hoped that his "hold-the-line" policy would help the country avoid hard economic times following World War II. The laws he wanted included controls on the wages workers earned and the profits companies could make. At the same time, the president also suggested a group of remarkable new laws designed to improve the lives of many Americans.

These laws called for new civil rights for minority groups, a national health plan system, and new federal aid to local schools. Thinking of the well-known "New Deal" of Franklin Roosevelt, Truman called his package of proposed new laws a "Fair Deal."

Unfortunately, Americans were not ready for the kinds of new laws Truman sought. During the war years, there were many new laws, some of them suggested by the Truman Committee, controlling the American economy. Now that the war was over, few business people or consumers were interested in still more controls. And although many of the "Fair Deal" laws Truman proposed were eventually passed under other presidents, especially Lyndon Johnson, Americans were not yet ready to accept them.

Congress failed to pass most of the new laws Truman proposed. And just as he had predicted, prices for consumer goods soared throughout much of 1946. Faced with a rising cost of living, many workers felt the need to earn more money.

In March of 1946, John L. Lewis, the leader of the United Mine Workers, led his union on strike, closing many coal mines throughout the nation. There was soon a coal shortage. This caused the lights in a number of major cities to be dimmed to conserve the electric power that was generated from coal. Soon railroad workers were threatening to go on strike too.

Truman solved both threats with strong, heavy-handed actions. First he seized control of the coal mines and forced a settlement of the strike. Then he threatened to draft railroad workers into the army if they left their jobs to go on strike. This forced them to stay on the job. The strike threat quickly ended.

Secretary of
Commerce Henry
Wallace signs the
resignation requested
by President Harry
Truman.

At the same time, some members of Truman's cabinet began acting on their own, disregarding the president's wishes. One of the biggest troublemakers was Secretary of State James Byrnes, the man who had asked Truman to nominate him for vice-president in 1944. Apparently, Byrnes still thought that he, not Truman, should have won the nomination. When President Truman asked Byrnes for a report of a Moscow meeting, Byrnes said that he was going to address the nation on radio and that the president could listen to his speech! Secretary of Commerce Henry Wallace, the man who had been Franklin Roosevelt's vice-president before Harry Truman, also caused no end of problems. Eventually, Truman had to fire Wallace and ask for Byrnes's resignation.

With the American economy in difficulty and his own cabinet rebelling against his authority, President Truman's popularity began to sink rapidly. Many Americans began to feel that he simply wasn't up to the difficult job of being president. Jokes about his work began to sweep across the nation. The old saying "To err is human" was modernized as "To err is Truman." One comic asked, "What would the President do if he were alive?"

Truman fought back hard against his critics, while at the same time trying to get the American people to help improve the nation's economy. He even began to use the new electronic marvel called television. On October 5, 1947, he made the first televised broadcast from the White House, asking Americans to conserve food. Unfortunately, television was not quite the power in 1947 that it is now. The broadcast was relayed only to New York City, Philadelphia, and the town of Schenectady, New York.

Despite his domestic problems, Truman kept a firm grasp on foreign affairs. In the summer of 1946, it became clear that the Soviet Union was interested in controlling more countries than those it had conquered near the end of World War II. The president was forced to send a fleet of navy ships to the ocean near Turkey to keep that country from being overrun by Russian soldiers. Early in 1947, Truman asked Congress for huge amounts of foreign aid to protect Greece and Turkey from attack by Russia. This policy of protecting free countries from Russia eventually became known as the "Truman Doctrine." To this day, the Truman Doctrine is an important element in the foreign policy of the U.S. government.

**Above: A French shirt factory that received aid through the Marshall Plan
Opposite page: Greece celebrates its millionth ton of Marshall Plan goods.**

Even by early 1948, nearly three years after the war in Europe had ended, the economies of many European nations remained wrecked by the war. President Truman knew that this was a dangerous situation. Besides the human misery caused by economic problems, nations filled with poor, unemployed people might turn in desperation to other forms of government, including socialism and Communism. On April 3, 1948, he signed the first of a series of laws designed to help the economies in Western Europe. Because the idea was first suggested by General George Marshall, who replaced James Byrnes as secretary of state, the project became known as the Marshall Plan. Over the years, the Marshall Plan gave more than $12 billion in economic assistance to the nations of Europe.

Truman and New York Governor Thomas E. Dewey

Despite his brilliant service to his country in foreign affairs, Americans had mixed feelings when Truman announced that he would be a candidate for the presidency in 1948. The feelings of Democrats ranged from shock and anger to sadness and depression. Truman, they felt, could not possibly beat a Republican candidate. Some southern Democrats did not like the president's views on civil rights. They named their own candidate for president, South Carolina Governor Strom Thurmond. Another group of Republicans preferred to see Henry Wallace as the presidential nominee. They, too, abandoned Truman.

As they gleefully watched the Democratic party fall apart, the Republicans once again nominated New York Governor Thomas E. Dewey as their candidate for president. Although Dewey had been defeated in 1944 by President Roosevelt, almost every political expert in America now agreed that the election was his.

An American plane flies food supplies into blockaded Berlin.

While all this was going on, the Russians handed Truman yet another problem. In June of 1948, Russian soldiers blocked the only highway leading into the German city of Berlin. Although Berlin was inside Communist-controlled East Germany, by agreement it remained non-Communist. Suddenly, there was no way for Western countries to bring food and supplies into the city. The Russians seemed to be ready to go to war, just waiting for the western nations to fire the first shots.

President Truman found a brilliant solution to the problem. Rather than challenge Russian soldiers, he sent airplanes carrying supplies into Berlin. It was expensive, but far cheaper than a military battle. Now, if the Russians wanted to go to war over control of Berlin, they would have to start it. They chose not to, giving up their blockade the following year.

Although most people thought he didn't have a chance to win, Harry Truman campaigned hard throughout the second half of 1948. Traveling in a special railroad car throughout much of the country, the president gave ringing speeches at every brief stop. Speaking from a little platform at the back of the car, he challenged the American people to think about the things he had done, and then to get out and vote. At some of the stops, listeners shouted, "Give 'em hell, Harry!"

Still, the polls showed Thomas Dewey and the Republicans had far more support than Truman among American citizens. When election day finally arrived on November 2, 1948, radio and newspaper reporters had already given the election to Dewey.

Like millions of other Americans, President Truman listened to radio reports as the ballots were counted on the night of November 2 and into the wee hours of the next day. "At 6 o'clock I was defeated," he said later. "At 10 o'clock I was defeated; 12 o'clock I was defeated; 4 o'clock I had won the election. And the next morning . . . in St. Louis, I was handed a paper which said, DEWEY DEFEATS TRUMAN! Of course, he wished he had, but he didn't and that's all there was to it."

By more than two million votes, Truman had defeated Thomas E. Dewey. In the counting of all-important electoral votes, Truman had won 303 to Dewey's 189, an easy victory. He had fooled all the experts and for the first time was elected president in his own right. For the first time, the presidential inauguration was covered by television. An estimated ten million American viewers watched the

The victorious Truman laughs as he holds up news of his defeat.

ceremony. The newspaper Truman referred to was the
Chicago Daily Tribune. The banner headline at the top of
page one of the November 3 edition read: "DEWEY
DEFEATS TRUMAN!" Many people still laugh at the huge
mistake the *Tribune* editors made so long ago.

Not so humorous was the growing feeling that
Americans were fighting a "Cold War" against Russia and
Communism. Although there were no armed battles as
there would be in a "hot" war, many Americans felt that
Communists would do anything to destroy the democratic
governments of America and Western Europe. And, they
feared, there were some Americans who would help them
do just that.

In 1948, the same year Truman won his only presidential election, ten Hollywood screenwriters were put in jail because they refused to answer questions put forward by members of the House Un-American Activities Committee. Members of the committee were trying to find Communists who might endanger the U.S. government. Instead, they bullied private citizens who had broken no laws, and some of them they sent to jail. President Truman called the committee's work the most "un-American activity in the whole government." But there was little he could do. The Cold War was raging, and some politicians found it convenient to believe that there were Communist spies hiding everywhere.

Less than two years later, however, people throughout America and the world learned that there were dangers from spies willing to help Communist governments. In February of 1950, a British scientist was arrested in England and confessed to giving secrets to the Russian government. As part of his confession, he also named several Americans who had given secrets about how to make atomic bombs to the Soviet government. The following year, two Americans named Julius and Ethel Rosenberg were sentenced to death, accused of giving top secret information to the Communists.

Even by early 1950, when the Rosenberg story was just appearing, the Cold War was becoming a hysteria. That year, a senator from Wisconsin named Joseph McCarthy seemed about to lose his bid for reelection. To attract more interest in his campaign, he began to accuse dozens and then hundreds of Americans of being Communists eager to

Julius and Ethel Rosenberg, who were executed for espionage

overthrow the government. Joseph McCarthy searched for Communists for years. He never proved that he had found a single one, but he caused many innocent victims great humiliation. Some even lost their jobs.

For his part, President Truman had no power to stop McCarthy's nasty work. Many congressmen, however, were greatly alarmed by McCarthy's unproven charges. In 1950, Congress passed a bill called the McCarren Act, which required all Communists in America to register with the U.S. Justice Department. Truman believed that the bill was ridiculous, saying that it was like passing a law to make "thieves report to the sheriff." But Congress managed to pass the law over Truman's veto. Fifteen years later, in 1965, the Supreme Court declared it unconstitutional.

Tanks roll through the streets of Seoul, South Korea.

While American politicians were searching everywhere for imagined Communists at home, real Communist soldiers were causing considerable problems abroad. On June 24, 1950, North Korean Communists crossed the thirty-eighth parallel, which divided the countries of North Korea and South Korea. Hours after the invasion, President Truman ordered American ships and planes to Korea to attempt to stop the invasion. Most of the important countries with representatives at the United Nations agreed with President Truman's actions. Russia did not, but since it was angry at the UN, it was not attending meetings and could not veto the UN decision.

General Douglas MacArthur (center) in South Korea

Other UN countries added their own soldiers to the American troops hurriedly traveling to Korea. Put in charge of all the UN forces was a hero from World War II, U.S. General Douglas MacArthur. From the very beginning, MacArthur and President Truman argued over how the war should be fought.

Truman, as well as many of America's top military leaders, knew that the Korean situation was a dangerous one. The two Koreas were very near both Russia and China. Russia, like North Korea, was a Communist nation. China had recently ended a long civil war and now it too was Communist. Only soldiers from Communist North Korea had invaded the south. Although both nations hoped the Communist soldiers from North Korea would win the war, neither Russia nor China had sent any soldiers to help them. Truman was anxious to see that they didn't.

Truman told General MacArthur to stay south of the thirty-eighth parallel. If he attacked North Korea, the president worried, the Russians or the Chinese might become alarmed and send their own troops into battle. Insisting that there was no danger from the huge countries to the north, General MacArthur sent his armies deep into North Korea.

General MacArthur was wrong. As his troops approached the Yalu River, which separated North Korea from China, a huge Chinese army, with support overhead from airplanes, attacked. MacArthur's soldiers were forced to retreat all the way back into South Korea. MacArthur wanted to attack airfields inside China, but Truman and the UN leadership disagreed. The war was rapidly getting out of hand.

When, in March of 1951, United Nations officials made a plan for peace, MacArthur decided to negotiate on his own with the Chinese. Although the U.S. Constitution clearly says that the president is the commander-in-chief of the American military, General MacArthur seemed to feel that he, and not the president, should be the real leader. Many Americans, remembering the general's brave leadership during World War II, seemed to agree with him. When Truman ordered him home and took away his command a few weeks later, some Americans were angered. Only later, when Senate hearings proved that MacArthur had acted improperly, did some people realize how wisely the president had acted. Nevertheless, a popular song during the 1952 presidential election year was entitled "General MacArthur for President."

Truman named General Matthew Ridgway (left) to succeed MacArthur (center).

President Truman was not able to end the Korean War. It continued until, under the administration of Dwight Eisenhower, a peace plan was reached that left the two countries as they were before the attack by North Korea. But the MacArthur affair made Harry Truman once again a controversial president. There were calls for his impeachment. He was sometimes booed in public. It would take some time for many people to realize that Truman had helped his country and much of the world through a difficult time.

In 1952, at the age of sixty-eight, President Truman decided not to run again for reelection. The administration of one of the country's most fascinating and decisive presidents had come to an end.

Chapter 6

Back Home in Independence

On January 21, 1953, the day after Dwight Eisenhower became the thirty-fourth president of the United States, Harry and Bess Truman arrived by train in Kansas City, just a few miles from Independence. When the train arrived at the station, a huge crowd of people had gathered to welcome home the retiring president and the former First Lady.

"I'm home for good and I mean it," Harry told the cheering crowd. And the people of western Missouri seemed happy to see their most famous citizen finally return. All along the short drive back to his home in Independence, people waved and cheered as his car drove by.

Harry Truman was no longer the president, but he was hardly finished working. He settled down to write two long books about his years in the White House. He called one, largely about his first twelve months in office, *Year of Decisions*. The other, *Years of Trial and Hope*, was about his remaining time as president. The books were extremely important additions to the subject of history that he loved so dearly. Many shorter books about his life draw much information from those two works.

Opposite page: Harry and Bess

Margaret and Bess watch Harry cut the cake on his seventieth birthday.

He also worked hard to establish the Truman Library in Independence. There, many official papers from his presidency, as well as some amusing souvenirs, are stored for future students of history to study.

For a number of years, he stayed out of the public limelight, driving each day to an office in town to work on his books and other projects. He rarely missed the opportunity to take morning walks as well. Neighbors frequently saw the former president, still walking briskly for a man in his seventies, out catching the morning air.

But even in retirement, Harry Truman still created controversy. In 1960, he campaigned for the Democratic presidential candidate, John F. Kennedy. He apparently had no love for the Republican candidate, Vice-President Richard Nixon. In San Antonio, he said that any Texan

Margaret, husband Clifton Daniel, Harry, Bess, and grandsons Clifton and Billy

who voted for Nixon should "go to hell." Nixon said that the former president's remark was a menace to children. Adult American voters nevertheless elected Kennedy.

Harry Truman died in 1972, at the age of eighty-eight, and was buried in the courtyard of the Truman Library. He had been involved in heated controversy throughout much of his political career. Although never afraid of the battles, he probably would have preferred to stay in the Senate for the rest of his career.

During the early years of his presidency, his press secretary, a childhood friend from Independence, once remarked that Harry would "rather be right than be President."

"I'd rather be anything than be President," Truman responded.

Harry Truman mixes with the stars—Opposite page: Playing the piano for actress Lauren Bacall and servicemen during the war. Above: Comedian George Jessel gives him a kiss on his eighty-second birthday.

Above: Truman, famous for his brisk morning walks, at the age of eighty-eight
Opposite page: Saluting a Fourth of July parade in Independence, Missouri, in 1971

Chronology of American History

(Shaded area covers events in Harry S. Truman's lifetime.)

About A.D. 982 — Eric the Red, born in Norway, reaches Greenland in one of the first European voyages to North America.

About 1000 — Leif Ericson (Eric the Red's son) leads what is thought to be the first European expedition to mainland North America; Leif probably lands in Canada.

1492 — Christopher Columbus, seeking a sea route from Spain to the Far East, discovers the New World.

1497 — John Cabot reaches Canada in the first English voyage to North America.

1513 — Ponce de Léon explores Florida in search of the fabled Fountain of Youth.

1519-1521 — Hernando Cortés of Spain conquers Mexico.

1534 — French explorers led by Jacques Cartier enter the Gulf of St. Lawrence in Canada.

1540 — Spanish explorer Francisco Coronado begins exploring the American Southwest, seeking the riches of the mythical Seven Cities of Cibola.

1565 — St. Augustine, Florida, the first permanent European town in what is now the United States, is founded by the Spanish.

1607 — Jamestown, Virginia, is founded, the first permanent English town in the present-day U.S.

1608 — Frenchman Samuel de Champlain founds the village of Quebec, Canada.

1609 — Henry Hudson explores the eastern coast of present-day U.S. for the Netherlands; the Dutch then claim parts of New York, New Jersey, Delaware, and Connecticut and name the area New Netherland.

1619 — The English colonies' first shipment of black slaves arrives in Jamestown.

1620 — English Pilgrims found Massachusetts' first permanent town at Plymouth.

1621 — Massachusetts Pilgrims and Indians hold the famous first Thanksgiving feast in colonial America.

1623 — Colonization of New Hampshire is begun by the English.

1624 — Colonization of present-day New York State is begun by the Dutch at Fort Orange (Albany).

1625 — The Dutch start building New Amsterdam (now New York City).

1630 — The town of Boston, Massachusetts, is founded by the English Puritans.

1633 — Colonization of Connecticut is begun by the English.

1634 — Colonization of Maryland is begun by the English.

1636 — Harvard, the colonies' first college, is founded in Massachusetts. Rhode Island colonization begins when Englishman Roger Williams founds Providence.

1638 — Delaware colonization begins as Swedes build Fort Christina at present-day Wilmington.

1640 — Stephen Daye of Cambridge, Massachusetts prints *The Bay Psalm Book*, the first English-language book published in what is now the U.S.

1643 — Swedish settlers begin colonizing Pennsylvania.

About 1650 — North Carolina is colonized by Virginia settlers.

1660 — New Jersey colonization is begun by the Dutch at present-day Jersey City.

1670 — South Carolina colonization is begun by the English near Charleston.

1673 — Jacques Marquette and Louis Jolliet explore the upper Mississippi River for France.

1682—Philadelphia, Pennsylvania, is settled. La Salle explores Mississippi River all the way to its mouth in Louisiana and claims the whole Mississippi Valley for France.

1693—College of William and Mary is founded in Williamsburg, Virginia.

1700—Colonial population is about 250,000.

1703—Benjamin Franklin is born in Boston.

1732—George Washington, first president of the U.S., is born in Westmoreland County, Virginia.

1733—James Oglethorpe founds Savannah, Georgia; Georgia is established as the thirteenth colony.

1735—John Adams, second president of the U.S., is born in Braintree, Massachusetts.

1737—William Byrd founds Richmond, Virginia.

1738—British troops are sent to Georgia over border dispute with Spain.

1739—Black insurrection takes place in South Carolina.

1740—English Parliament passes act allowing naturalization of immigrants to American colonies after seven-year residence.

1743—Thomas Jefferson is born in Albemarle County, Virginia. Benjamin Franklin retires at age thirty-seven to devote himself to scientific inquiries and public service.

1744—King George's War begins; France joins war effort against England.

1745—During King George's War, France raids settlements in Maine and New York.

1747—Classes begin at Princeton College in New Jersey.

1748—The Treaty of Aix-la-Chapelle concludes King George's War.

1749—Parliament legally recognizes slavery in colonies and the inauguration of the plantation system in the South. George Washington becomes the surveyor for Culpepper County in Virginia.

1750—Thomas Walker passes through and names Cumberland Gap on his way toward Kentucky region. Colonial population is about 1,200,000.

1751—James Madison, fourth president of the U.S., is born in Port Conway, Virginia. English Parliament passes Currency Act, banning New England colonies from issuing paper money. George Washington travels to Barbados.

1752—Pennsylvania Hospital, the first general hospital in the colonies, is founded in Philadelphia. Benjamin Franklin uses a kite in a thunderstorm to demonstrate that lightning is a form of electricity.

1753—George Washington delivers command that the French withdraw from the Ohio River Valley; French disregard the demand. Colonial population is about 1,328,000.

1754—French and Indian War begins (extends to Europe as the Seven Years' War). Washington surrenders at Fort Necessity.

1755—French and Indians ambush Braddock. Washington becomes commander of Virginia troops.

1756—England declares war on France.

1758—James Monroe, fifth president of the U.S., is born in Westmoreland County, Virginia.

1759—Cherokee Indian war begins in southern colonies; hostilities extend to 1761. George Washington marries Martha Dandridge Custis.

1760—George III becomes king of England. Colonial population is about 1,600,000.

1762—England declares war on Spain.

1763—Treaty of Paris concludes the French and Indian War and the Seven Years' War. England gains Canada and most other French lands east of the Mississippi River.

1764—British pass the Sugar Act to gain tax money from the colonists. The issue of taxation without representation is first introduced in Boston. John Adams marries Abigail Smith.

1765—Stamp Act goes into effect in the colonies. Business virtually stops as almost all colonists refuse to use the stamps.

1766—British repeal the Stamp Act.

1767—John Quincy Adams, sixth president of the U.S. and son of second president John Adams, is born in Braintree, Massachusetts. Andrew Jackson, seventh president of the U.S., is born in Waxhaw settlement, South Carolina.

1769—Daniel Boone sights the Kentucky Territory.

1770—In the Boston Massacre, British soldiers kill five colonists and injure six. Townshend Acts are repealed, thus eliminating all duties on imports to the colonies except tea.

1771—Benjamin Franklin begins his autobiography, a work that he will never complete. The North Carolina assembly passes the "Bloody Act," which makes rioters guilty of treason.

1772—Samuel Adams rouses colonists to consider British threats to self-government.

1773—English Parliament passes the Tea Act. Colonists dressed as Mohawk Indians board British tea ships and toss 342 casks of tea into the water in what becomes known as the Boston Tea Party. William Henry Harrison is born in Charles City County, Virginia.

1774—British close the port of Boston to punish the city for the Boston Tea Party. First Continental Congress convenes in Philadelphia.

1775—American Revolution begins with battles of Lexington and Concord, Massachusetts. Second Continental Congress opens in Philadelphia. George Washington becomes commander-in-chief of the Continental army.

1776—Declaration of Independence is adopted on July 4.

1777—Congress adopts the American flag with thirteen stars and thirteen stripes. John Adams is sent to France to negotiate peace treaty.

1778—France declares war against Great Britain and becomes U.S. ally.

1779—British surrender to Americans at Vincennes. Thomas Jefferson is elected governor of Virginia. James Madison is elected to the Continental Congress.

1780—Benedict Arnold, first American traitor, defects to the British.

1781—Articles of Confederation go into effect. Cornwallis surrenders to George Washington at Yorktown, ending the American Revolution.

1782—American commissioners, including John Adams, sign peace treaty with British in Paris. Thomas Jefferson's wife, Martha, dies. Martin Van Buren is born in Kinderhook, New York.

1784—Zachary Taylor is born near Barboursville, Virginia.

1785—Congress adopts the dollar as the unit of currency. John Adams is made minister to Great Britain. Thomas Jefferson is appointed minister to France.

1786—Shays's Rebellion begins in Massachusetts.

1787—Constitutional Convention assembles in Philadelphia, with George Washington presiding; U.S. Constitution is adopted. Delaware, New Jersey, and Pennsylvania become states.

1788—Virginia, South Carolina, New York, Connecticut, New Hampshire, Maryland, and Massachusetts become states. U.S. Constitution is ratified. New York City is declared U.S. capital.

1789—Presidential electors elect George Washington and John Adams as first president and vice-president. Thomas Jefferson is appointed secretary of state. North Carolina becomes a state. French Revolution begins.

1790—Supreme Court meets for the first time. Rhode Island becomes a state. First national census in the U.S. counts 3,929,214 persons. John Tyler is born in Charles City County, Virginia.

1791—Vermont enters the Union. U.S. Bill of Rights, the first ten amendments to the Constitution, goes into effect. District of Columbia is established. James Buchanan is born in Stony Batter, Pennsylvania.

1792—Thomas Paine publishes *The Rights of Man*. Kentucky becomes a state. Two political parties are formed in the U.S., Federalist and Republican. Washington is elected to a second term, with Adams as vice-president.

1793—War between France and Britain begins; U.S. declares neutrality. Eli Whitney invents the cotton gin; cotton production and slave labor increase in the South.

1794—Eleventh Amendment to the Constitution is passed, limiting federal courts' power. "Whiskey Rebellion" in Pennsylvania protests federal whiskey tax. James Madison marries Dolley Payne Todd.

1795—George Washington signs the Jay Treaty with Great Britain. Treaty of San Lorenzo, between U.S. and Spain, settles Florida boundary and gives U.S. right to navigate the Mississippi. James Polk is born near Pineville, North Carolina.

1796—Tennessee enters the Union. Washington gives his Farewell Address, refusing a third presidential term. John Adams is elected president and Thomas Jefferson vice-president.

1797—Adams recommends defense measures against possible war with France. Napoleon Bonaparte and his army march against Austrians in Italy. U.S. population is about 4,900,000.

1798—Washington is named commander-in-chief of the U.S. Army. Department of the Navy is created. Alien and Sedition Acts are passed. Napoleon's troops invade Egypt and Switzerland.

1799—George Washington dies at Mount Vernon, New York. James Monroe is elected governor of Virginia. French Revolution ends. Napoleon becomes ruler of France.

1800—Thomas Jefferson and Aaron Burr tie for president. U.S. capital is moved from Philadelphia to Washington, D.C. The White House is built as presidents' home. Spain returns Louisiana to France. Millard Fillmore is born in Locke, New York.

1801—After thirty-six ballots, House of Representatives elects Thomas Jefferson president, making Burr vice-president. James Madison is named secretary of state.

1802—Congress abolishes excise taxes. U.S. Military Academy is founded at West Point, New York.

1803—Ohio enters the Union. Louisiana Purchase treaty is signed with France, greatly expanding U.S. territory.

1804—Twelfth Amendment to the Constitution rules that president and vice-president be elected separately. Alexander Hamilton is killed by Vice-President Aaron Burr in a duel. Orleans Territory is established. Napoleon crowns himself emperor of France. Franklin Pierce is born in Hillsborough Lower Village, New Hampshire.

1805—Thomas Jefferson begins his second term as president. Lewis and Clark expedition reaches the Pacific Ocean.

1806—Coinage of silver dollars is stopped; resumes in 1836.

1807—Aaron Burr is acquitted in treason trial. Embargo Act closes U.S. ports to trade.

1808—James Madison is elected president. Congress outlaws importing slaves from Africa. Andrew Johnson is born in Raleigh, North Carolina.

1809—Abraham Lincoln is born near Hodgenville, Kentucky.

1810—U.S. population is 7,240,000.

1811—William Henry Harrison defeats Indians at Tippecanoe. Monroe is named secretary of state.

1812—Louisiana becomes a state. U.S. declares war on Britain (War of 1812). James Madison is reelected president. Napoleon invades Russia.

1813—British forces take Fort Niagara and Buffalo, New York.

1814—Francis Scott Key writes "The Star-Spangled Banner." British troops burn much of Washington, D.C., including the White House. Treaty of Ghent ends War of 1812. James Monroe becomes secretary of war.

1815—Napoleon meets his final defeat at Battle of Waterloo.

1816—James Monroe is elected president. Indiana becomes a state.

1817—Mississippi becomes a state. Construction on Erie Canal begins.

1818—Illinois enters the Union. The present thirteen-stripe flag is adopted. Border between U.S. and Canada is agreed upon.

1819—Alabama becomes a state. U.S. purchases Florida from Spain. Thomas Jefferson establishes the University of Virginia.

1820—James Monroe is reelected. In the Missouri Compromise, Maine enters the Union as a free (non-slave) state.

1821—Missouri enters the Union as a slave state. Santa Fe Trail opens the American Southwest. Mexico declares independence from Spain. Napoleon Bonaparte dies.

1822—U.S. recognizes Mexico and Colombia. Liberia in Africa is founded as a home for freed slaves. Ulysses S. Grant is born in Point Pleasant, Ohio. Rutherford B. Hayes is born in Delaware, Ohio.

1823—Monroe Doctrine closes North and South America to European colonizing or invasion.

1824—House of Representatives elects John Quincy Adams president when none of the four candidates wins a majority in national election. Mexico becomes a republic.

1825—Erie Canal is opened. U.S. population is 11,300,000.

1826—Thomas Jefferson and John Adams both die on July 4, the fiftieth anniversary of the Declaration of Independence.

1828—Andrew Jackson is elected president. Tariff of Abominations is passed, cutting imports.

1829—James Madison attends Virginia's constitutional convention. Slavery is abolished in Mexico. Chester A. Arthur is born in Fairfield, Vermont.

1830—Indian Removal Act to resettle Indians west of the Mississippi is approved.

1831—James Monroe dies in New York City. James A. Garfield is born in Orange, Ohio. Cyrus McCormick develops his reaper.

1832—Andrew Jackson, nominated by the new Democratic Party, is reelected president.

1833—Britain abolishes slavery in its colonies. Benjamin Harrison is born in North Bend, Ohio.

1835—Federal government becomes debt-free for the first time.

1836—Martin Van Buren becomes president. Texas wins independence from Mexico. Arkansas joins the Union. James Madison dies at Montpelier, Virginia.

1837—Michigan enters the Union. U.S. population is 15,900,000. Grover Cleveland is born in Caldwell, New Jersey.

1840—William Henry Harrison is elected president.

1841—President Harrison dies in Washington, D.C., one month after inauguration. Vice-President John Tyler succeeds him.

1843—William McKinley is born in Niles, Ohio.

1844—James Knox Polk is elected president. Samuel Morse sends first telegraphic message.

1845—Texas and Florida become states. Potato famine in Ireland causes massive emigration from Ireland to U.S. Andrew Jackson dies near Nashville, Tennessee.

1846—Iowa enters the Union. War with Mexico begins.

1847—U.S. captures Mexico City.

1848—Zachary Taylor becomes president. Treaty of Guadalupe Hidalgo ends Mexico-U.S. war. Wisconsin becomes a state.

1849—James Polk dies in Nashville, Tennessee.

1850—President Taylor dies in Washington, D.C.; Vice-President Millard Fillmore succeeds him. California enters the Union, breaking tie between slave and free states.

1852—Franklin Pierce is elected president.

1853—Gadsden Purchase transfers Mexican territory to U.S.

1854—"War for Bleeding Kansas" is fought between slave and free states.

1855—Czar Nicholas I of Russia dies, succeeded by Alexander II.

1856—James Buchanan is elected president. In Massacre of Potawatomi Creek, Kansas-slavers are murdered by free-staters. Woodrow Wilson is born in Staunton, Pennsylvania.

1857—William Howard Taft is born in Cincinnati, Ohio.

1858—Minnesota enters the Union. Theodore Roosevelt is born in New York City.

1859—Oregon becomes a state.

1860—Abraham Lincoln is elected president; South Carolina secedes from the Union in protest.

1861—Arkansas, Tennessee, North Carolina, and Virginia secede. Kansas enters the Union as a free state. Civil War begins.

1862—Union forces capture Fort Henry, Roanoke Island, Fort Donelson, Jacksonville, and New Orleans; Union armies are defeated at the battles of Bull Run and Fredericksburg. Martin Van Buren dies in Kinderhook, New York. John Tyler dies near Charles City, Virginia.

1863—Lincoln issues Emancipation Proclamation: all slaves held in rebelling territories are declared free. West Virginia becomes a state.

1864—Abraham Lincoln is reelected. Nevada becomes a state.

1865—Lincoln is assassinated in Washington, D.C., and succeeded by Andrew Johnson. U.S. Civil War ends on May 26. Thirteenth Amendment abolishes slavery. Warren G. Harding is born in Blooming Grove, Ohio.

1867—Nebraska becomes a state. U.S. buys Alaska from Russia for $7,200,000. Reconstruction Acts are passed.

1868—President Johnson is impeached for violating Tenure of Office Act, but is acquitted by Senate. Ulysses S. Grant is elected president. Fourteenth Amendment prohibits voting discrimination. James Buchanan dies in Lancaster, Pennsylvania.

1869—Franklin Pierce dies in Concord, New Hampshire.

1870—Fifteenth Amendment gives blacks the right to vote.

1872—Grant is reelected over Horace Greeley. General Amnesty Act pardons ex-Confederates. Calvin Coolidge is born in Plymouth Notch, Vermont.

1874—Millard Fillmore dies in Buffalo, New York. Herbert Hoover is born in West Branch, Iowa.

1875—Andrew Johnson dies in Carter's Station, Tennessee.

1876—Colorado enters the Union. "Custer's last stand": he and his men are massacred by Sioux Indians at Little Big Horn, Montana.

1877—Rutherford B. Hayes is elected president as all disputed votes are awarded to him.

1880—James A. Garfield is elected president.

1881—President Garfield is assassinated and dies in Elberon, New Jersey. Vice-President Chester A. Arthur succeeds him.

1882—U.S. bans Chinese immigration. Franklin D. Roosevelt is born in Hyde Park, New York.

1884—Grover Cleveland is elected president. Harry S. Truman is born in Lamar, Missouri.

1885—Ulysses S. Grant dies in Mount McGregor, New York.

1886—Statue of Liberty is dedicated. Chester A. Arthur dies in New York City.

1888—Benjamin Harrison is elected president.

1889—North Dakota, South Dakota, Washington, and Montana become states.

1890—Dwight D. Eisenhower is born in Denison, Texas. Idaho and Wyoming become states.

1892—Grover Cleveland is elected president.

1893—Rutherford B. Hayes dies in Fremont, Ohio.

1896—William McKinley is elected president. Utah becomes a state.

1898—U.S. declares war on Spain over Cuba.

1900—McKinley is reelected. Boxer Rebellion against foreigners in China begins.

1901—McKinley is assassinated by anarchist Leon Czolgosz in Buffalo, New York; Theodore Roosevelt becomes president. Benjamin Harrison dies in Indianapolis, Indiana.

1902—U.S. acquires perpetual control over Panama Canal.

1903—Alaskan frontier is settled.

1904—Russian-Japanese War breaks out. Theodore Roosevelt wins presidential election.

1905—Treaty of Portsmouth signed, ending Russian-Japanese War.

1906—U.S. troops occupy Cuba.

1907—President Roosevelt bars all Japanese immigration. Oklahoma enters the Union.

1908—William Howard Taft becomes president. Grover Cleveland dies in Princeton, New Jersey. Lyndon B. Johnson is born near Stonewall, Texas.

1909—NAACP is founded under W.E.B. DuBois

1910—China abolishes slavery.

1911—Chinese Revolution begins. Ronald Reagan is born in Tampico, Illinois.

1912—Woodrow Wilson is elected president. Arizona and New Mexico become states.

1913—Federal income tax is introduced in U.S. through the Sixteenth Amendment. Richard Nixon is born in Yorba Linda, California. Gerald Ford is born in Omaha, Nebraska.

1914—World War I begins.

1915—British liner *Lusitania* is sunk by German submarine.

1916—Wilson is reelected president.

1917—U.S. breaks diplomatic relations with Germany. Czar Nicholas of Russia abdicates as revolution begins. U.S. declares war on Austria-Hungary. John F. Kennedy is born in Brookline, Massachusetts.

1918—Wilson proclaims "Fourteen Points" as war aims. On November 11, armistice is signed between Allies and Germany.

1919—Eighteenth Amendment prohibits sale and manufacture of intoxicating liquors. Wilson presides over first League of Nations; wins Nobel Peace Prize. Theodore Roosevelt dies in Oyster Bay, New York.

1920—Nineteenth Amendment (women's suffrage) is passed. Warren Harding is elected president.

1921—Adolf Hitler's stormtroopers begin to terrorize political opponents.

1922—Irish Free State is established. Soviet states form USSR. Benito Mussolini forms Fascist government in Italy.

1923—President Harding dies in San Francisco, California; he is succeeded by Vice-President Calvin Coolidge.

1924—Coolidge is elected president. Woodrow Wilson dies in Washington, D.C. James Carter is born in Plains, Georgia. George Bush is born in Milton, Massachusetts.

1925—Hitler reorganizes Nazi Party and publishes first volume of *Mein Kampf.*

1926—Fascist youth organizations founded in Germany and Italy. Republic of Lebanon proclaimed.

1927—Stalin becomes Soviet dictator. Economic conference in Geneva attended by fifty-two nations.

1928—Herbert Hoover is elected president. U.S. and many other nations sign Kellogg-Briand pacts to outlaw war.

1929—Stock prices in New York crash on "Black Thursday"; the Great Depression begins.

1930—Bank of U.S. and its many branches close (most significant bank failure of the year). William Howard Taft dies in Washington, D.C.

1931—Emigration from U.S. exceeds immigration for first time as Depression deepens.

1932—Franklin D. Roosevelt wins presidential election in a Democratic landslide.

1933—First concentration camps are erected in Germany. U.S. recognizes USSR and resumes trade. Twenty-First Amendment repeals prohibition. Calvin Coolidge dies in Northampton, Massachusetts.

1934—Severe dust storms hit Plains states. President Roosevelt passes U.S. Social Security Act.

1936—Roosevelt is reelected. Spanish Civil War begins. Hitler and Mussolini form Rome-Berlin Axis.

1937—Roosevelt signs Neutrality Act.

1938—Roosevelt sends appeal to Hitler and Mussolini to settle European problems amicably.

1939—Germany takes over Czechoslovakia and invades Poland, starting World War II.

1940—Roosevelt is reelected for a third term.

1941—Japan bombs Pearl Harbor, U.S. declares war on Japan. Germany and Italy declare war on U.S.; U.S. then declares war on them.

1942—Allies agree not to make separate peace treaties with the enemies. U.S. government transfers more than 100,000 Nisei (Japanese-Americans) from west coast to inland concentration camps.

1943—Allied bombings of Germany begin.

1944—Roosevelt is reelected for a fourth term. Allied forces invade Normandy on D-Day.

1945—President Franklin D. Roosevelt dies in Warm Springs, Georgia; Vice-President Harry S. Truman succeeds him. Mussolini is killed; Hitler commits suicide. Germany surrenders. U.S. drops atomic bomb on Hiroshima; Japan surrenders: end of World War II.

1946—U N General Assembly holds its first session in London. Peace conference of twenty-one nations is held in Paris.

1947—Peace treaties are signed in Paris. "Cold War" is in full swing.

1948—U.S. passes Marshall Plan Act, providing $17 billion in aid for Europe. U.S. recognizes new nation of Israel. India and Pakistan become free of British rule. Truman is elected president.

1949—Republic of Eire is proclaimed in Dublin. Russia blocks land route access from Western Germany to Berlin; airlift begins. U.S., France, and Britain agree to merge their zones of occupation in West Germany. Apartheid program begins in South Africa.

1950—Riots in Johannesburg, South Africa, against apartheid. North Korea invades South Korea. U.N. forces land in South Korea and recapture Seoul.

1951—Twenty-Second Amendment limits president to two terms.

1952—Dwight D. Eisenhower resigns as supreme commander in Europe and is elected president.

1953—Stalin dies; struggle for power in Russia follows. Rosenbergs are executed for espionage.

1954—U.S. and Japan sign mutual defense agreement.

1955—Blacks in Montgomery, Alabama, boycott segregated bus lines.

1956—Eisenhower is reelected president. Soviet troops march into Hungary.

1957—U.S. agrees to withdraw ground forces from Japan. Russia launches first satellite, *Sputnik.*

1958—European Common Market comes into being. Fidel Castro begins war against Batista government in Cuba.

1959—Alaska becomes the forty-ninth state. Hawaii becomes fiftieth state. Castro becomes premier of Cuba. De Gaulle is proclaimed president of the Fifth Republic of France.

1960—Historic debates between Senator John F. Kennedy and Vice-President Richard Nixon are televised. Kennedy is elected president. Brezhnev becomes president of USSR.

1961—Berlin Wall is constructed. Kennedy and Khrushchev confer in Vienna. In Bay of Pigs incident, Cubans trained by CIA attempt to overthrow Castro.

1962—U.S. military council is established in South Vietnam.

1963—Riots and beatings by police and whites mark civil rights demonstrations in Birmingham, Alabama; 30,000 troops are called out, Martin Luther King, Jr., is arrested. Freedom marchers descend on Washington, D.C., to demonstrate. President Kennedy is assassinated in Dallas, Texas; Vice-President Lyndon B. Johnson is sworn in as president.

1964—U.S. aircraft bomb North Vietnam. Johnson is elected president. Herbert Hoover dies in New York City.

1965—U.S. combat troops arrive in South Vietnam.

1966—Thousands protest U.S. policy in Vietnam. National Guard quells race riots in Chicago.

1967—Six-Day War between Israel and Arab nations.

1968—Martin Luther King, Jr., is assassinated in Memphis, Tennessee. Senator Robert Kennedy is assassinated in Los Angeles. Riots and police brutality take place at Democratic National Convention in Chicago. Richard Nixon is elected president. Czechoslovakia is invaded by Soviet troops.

1969—Dwight D. Eisenhower dies in Washington, D.C. Hundreds of thousands of people in several U.S. cities demonstrate against Vietnam War.

1970—Four Vietnam War protesters are killed by National Guardsmen at Kent State University in Ohio.

1971—Twenty-Sixth Amendment allows eighteen-year-olds to vote.

1972—Nixon visits Communist China; is reelected president in near-record landslide. Watergate affair begins when five men are arrested in the Watergate hotel complex in Washington, D.C. Nixon announces resignations of aides Haldeman, Ehrlichman, and Dean and Attorney General Kleindienst as a result of Watergate-related charges. Harry S. Truman dies in Kansas City, Missouri.

1973—Vice-President Spiro Agnew resigns; Gerald Ford is named vice-president. Vietnam peace treaty is formally approved after nineteen months of negotiations. Lyndon B. Johnson dies in San Antonio, Texas.

1974—As a result of Watergate cover-up, impeachment is considered; Nixon resigns and Ford becomes president. Ford pardons Nixon and grants limited amnesty to Vietnam War draft evaders and military deserters.

1975—U.S. civilians are evacuated from Saigon, South Vietnam, as Communist forces complete takeover of South Vietnam.

1976—U.S. celebrates its Bicentennial. James Earl Carter becomes president.

1977—Carter pardons most Vietnam draft evaders, numbering some 10,000.

1980—Ronald Reagan is elected president.

1981—President Reagan is shot in the chest in assassination attempt. Sandra Day O'Connor is appointed first woman justice of the Supreme Court.

1983—U.S. troops invade island of Grenada.

1984—Reagan is reelected president. Democratic candidate Walter Mondale's running mate, Geraldine Ferraro, is the first woman selected for vice-president by a major U.S. political party.

1985—Soviet Communist Party secretary Konstantin Chernenko dies; Mikhail Gorbachev succeeds him. U.S. and Soviet officials discuss arms control in Geneva. Reagan and Gorbachev hold summit conference in Geneva. Racial tensions accelerate in South Africa.

1986—Space shuttle *Challenger* explodes shortly after takeoff; crew of seven dies. U.S. bombs bases in Libya. Corazon Aquino defeats Ferdinand Marcos in Philippine presidential election.

1987—Iraqi missile rips the U.S. frigate *Stark* in the Persian Gulf, killing thirty-seven American sailors. Congress holds hearings to investigate sale of U.S. arms to Iran to finance Nicaraguan *contra* movement.

1988—George Bush is elected president. President Reagan and Soviet leader Gorbachev sign INF treaty, eliminating intermediate nuclear forces. Severe drought sweeps the United States.

1989—East Germany opens Berlin Wall, allowing citizens free exit. Communists lose control of governments in Poland, Rumania, and Czechoslovakia. Chinese troops massacre over 1,000 pro-democracy student demonstrators in Beijing's Tiananmen Square.

Index

Page numbers in boldface type indicate illustrations.

About the Author

   Jim Hargrove has worked as a wrtier and editor for more than ten years. After serving as an editorial director for three Chicago area publishers, he began a career as an independent writer, preparing a series of books for children. He has contributed to works by nearly twenty different publishers. His Childrens Press titles include biographies of Mark Twain and Richard Nixon. With his wife and daughter, he lives in a small Illinois town near the Wisconsin border.